Help the Black Rhinoceros

by Grace Hansen

Little Activists: Endangered Species
Abdo Kids

Abdo Kids Jumbo is an Imprint of Abdo Kids
abdobooks.com

abdobooks.com

Published by Abdo Kids, a division of ABDO, P.O. Box 398166, Minneapolis, Minnesota 55439.
Copyright © 2019 by Abdo Consulting Group, Inc. International copyrights reserved in all countries.
No part of this book may be reproduced in any form without written permission from the publisher.
Abdo Kids Jumbo™ is a trademark and logo of Abdo Kids.

102018
012019

THIS BOOK CONTAINS RECYCLED MATERIALS

Photo Credits: Getty Images, iStock, Shutterstock

Production Contributors: Teddy Borth, Jennie Forsberg, Grace Hansen

Design Contributors: Dorothy Toth, Laura Mitchell

Library of Congress Control Number: 2018946050
Publisher's Cataloging-in-Publication Data

Names: Hansen, Grace, author.
Title: Help the black rhinoceros / by Grace Hansen.
Description: Minneapolis, Minnesota : Abdo Kids, 2019 | Series: Little activists: endangered species | Includes glossary, index and online resources (page 24).
Identifiers: ISBN 9781532181986 (lib. bdg.) | ISBN 9781532182969 (ebook) | ISBN 9781532183454 (Read-to-me ebook)
Subjects: LCSH: Black rhinoceros--Juvenile literature. | Wildlife recovery--Juvenile literature. | Endangered species--Juvenile literature. | Rhinoceroses--Juvenile literature.
Classification: DDC 333.954--dc23

Table of Contents

Black Rhinos................4

Status....................10

Threats...................14

Why They Matter...........20

Black Rhinoceros Overview....22

Glossary..................23

Index.....................24

Abdo Kids Code............24

Black Rhinos

Black Rhinoceroses live in parts of Africa. They are gray in color. Most have two horns that can grow quite long!

5

Rhinos are some of the oldest mammal groups on the planet. Their ancestors lived more than 50 million years ago.

7

Today's rhinos are much smaller than their giant **ancestors**. Though they can still weigh a whopping 4,000 pounds (1,814 kg)!

9

Status

In Africa, around 5,400 black rhinos roam the savannas. These rhinos are considered **critically endangered**.

11

Today looks better than the year 1995. Then, there were only 2,500 black rhinos left in the wild. Protecting them became necessary.

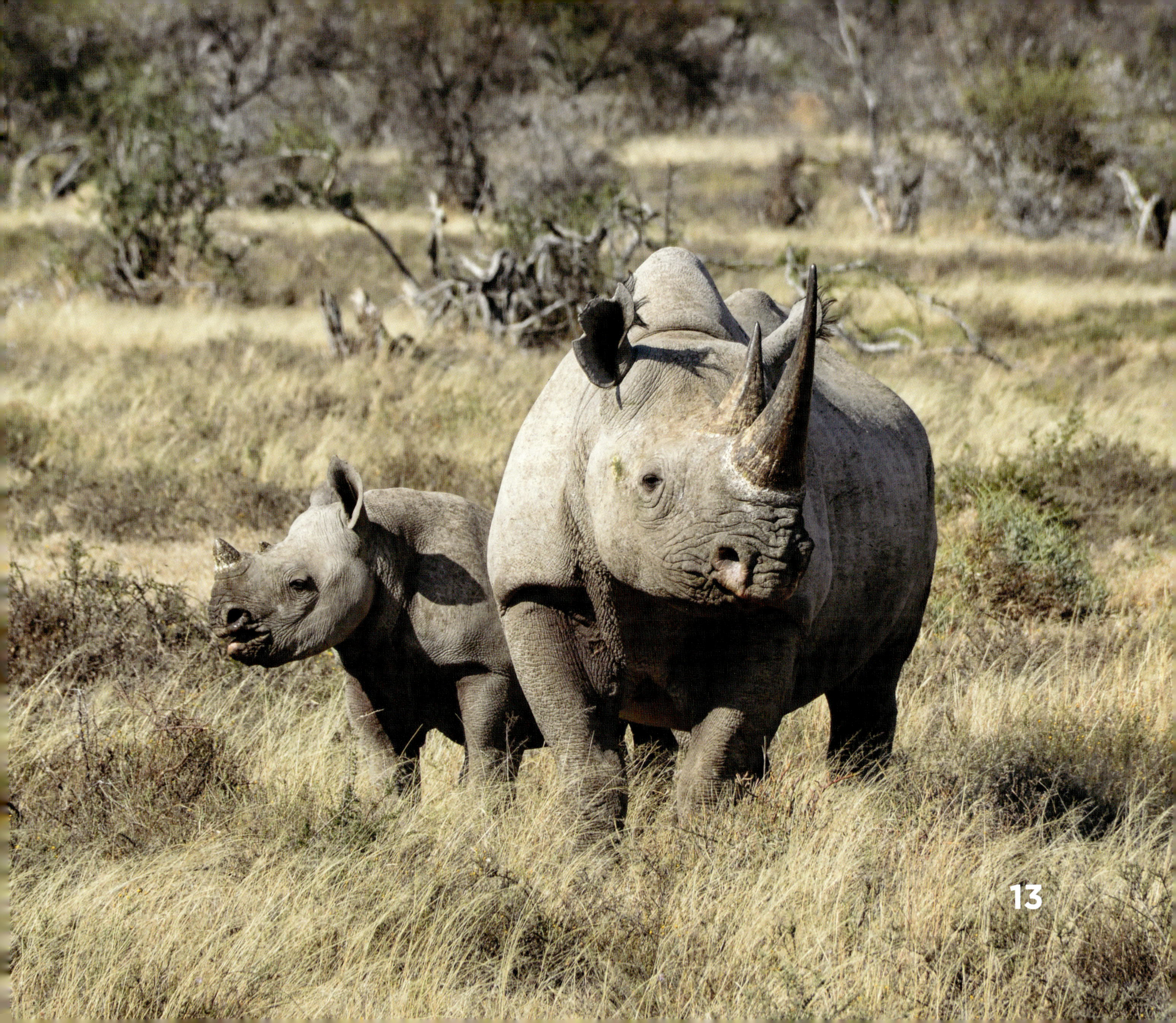

Threats

Habitat loss is one reason populations went down. Rhinos are very large and need to eat a lot of plants. The less space they have, the less food there is.

15

Rhinos also spend most of their lives alone. They need lots of room to roam.

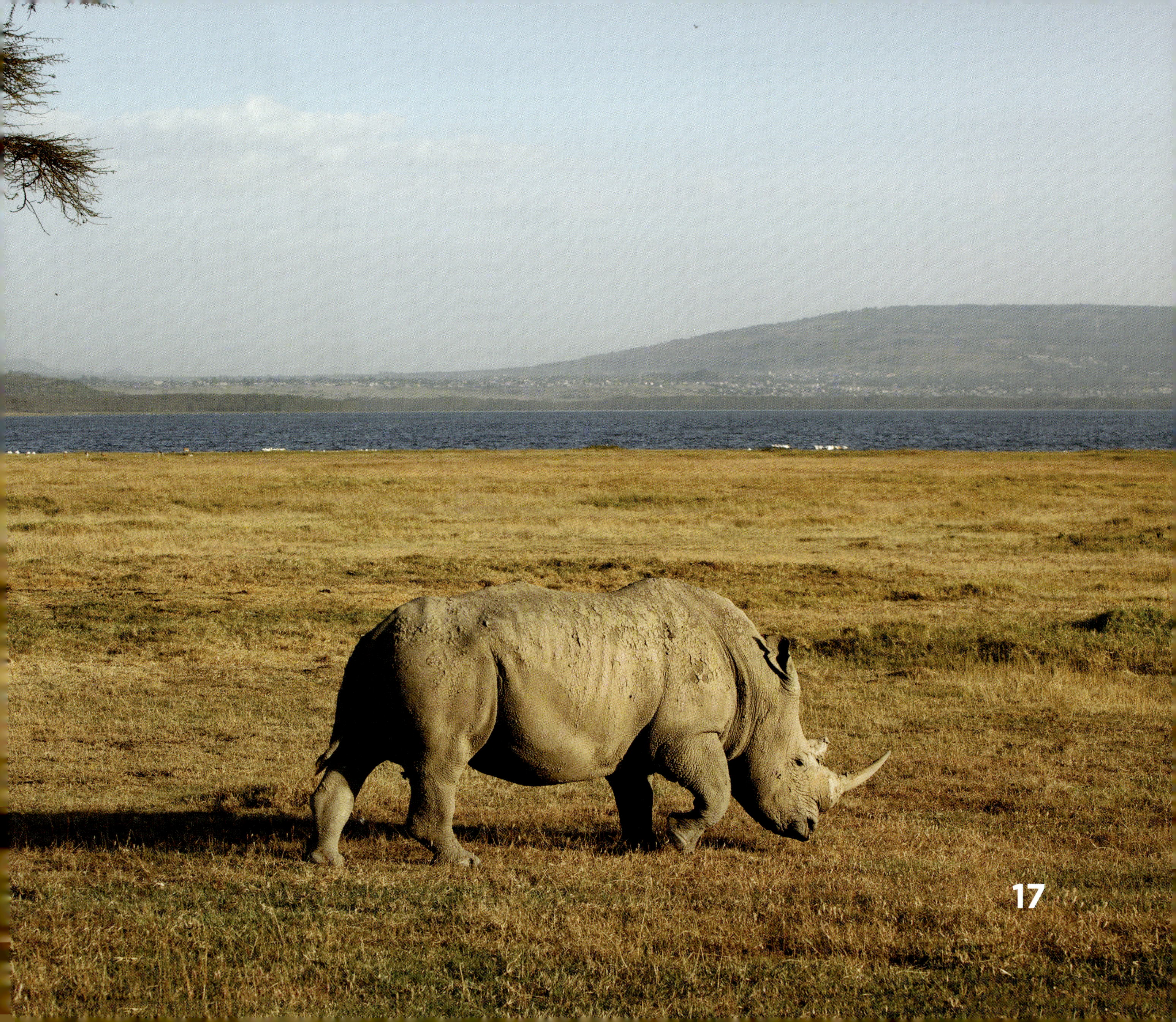

Poaching is the rhino's greatest threat. Many rhinos are killed each year for their horns. Rhino horns are prized in some cultures.

19

Why They Matter

Rhinos are very important to their habitats. Large blocks of land have been set aside to protect them. This has also helped other amazing African animals, like elephants.

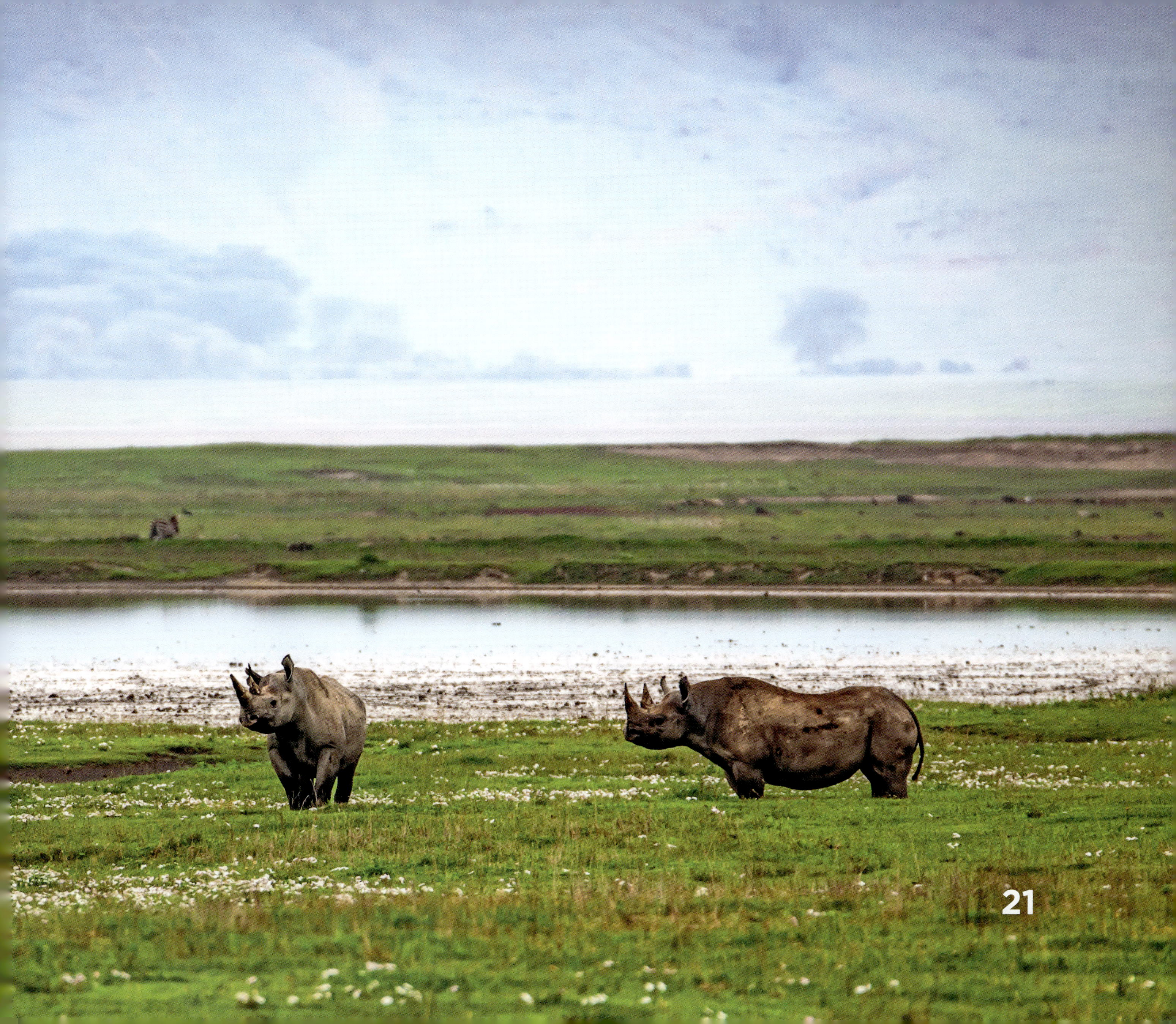

Black Rhinoceros Overview

- Status: **Critically Endangered**

- Population: 5,000–5,500

- Habitat: Grasslands, savannas, shrublands, and deserts in southern and eastern Africa

- Greatest Threats: **Poaching** and habitat loss

Glossary

ancestor – family members that lived a long time ago.

critically endangered – in extremely high danger of becoming extinct.

mammal – a warm-blooded animal with fur or hair on its skin and a skeleton inside its body. Mother mammals make milk for their babies.

poaching – hunting or trapping illegally.

Index

Africa 4, 10, 20

African elephant 20

ancestors 6, 8

color 4

food 14

habitat 4, 10, 14, 20

horns 4, 18

population 10, 12

protection 20

size 8, 14

threats 14, 18

weight 8

Abdo Kids ONLINE
FREE! ONLINE MULTIMEDIA RESOURCES

Visit **abdokids.com** and use this code to access crafts, games, videos, and more!

Abdo Kids Code:
LHK1986